Waking in Waikato

Angus Calder

diehard
Edinburgh

diehard
publishers
3 Spittal Street
Edinburgh
EH3 9DY

ISBN 0 946230 42 0
© Angus Calder 1997

British Library Cataloguing in Publication Data
A catalog record for this book is
available from the British Library

The Publisher acknowledges the financial assistance of the
Scottish Arts Council in the publication of this volume.

*other **diehard** poetry*

Richard Livermore, *The Divine Joker*,
Meltdown.
Colin Will, *Thirteen Ways of Looking at the Highlands*.
Martha Modena Vertreace, *Light Caught Bending*,
Second Mourning.
Stuart A. Paterson, *Saving Graces*.
Morelle Smith, *Deepwater Terminal*.
Sally Evans, *Millennial*.
Bashabi Fraser, *Life*.

*to my three
very grown up children:
Rachel, Gowan and Gideon*

This is Angus Calder's first book of poems. As a historian and writer on literature, culture and politics he has published, edited and contributed to many other books including the following:
The People's War: Britain 1939-1945 (Pimlico)
Revolutionary Empire (Pimlico)
The Myth of the Blitz (Pimlico)
Revolving Culture: Notes from the Scottish Republic
(I.B. Tauris)
His next books are an edition for Penguin of *Selected Poems* by R L Stevenson and Volumes 2 and 3 of *The Raucle Tongue: Hitherto Uncollected Prose* of Hugh MacDiarmid, edited with Glen Murray and Alan Riach for Carcanet.

Of the "Autumn Poems", "Border" was in the first issue of *Inter Arts*, "Soft Fruit Above Forfar" appeared in *Lines Review*, "September Starting" in *New Writing Scotland 1994*, "Crab" appeared in *New Statesman and New Poems 1967 (Hutchinson)*, "On the Far Side" in *Edinburgh University History Graduates Newsletter* and "November Nature" in *Proteus*. "Curling: Old Murrayfield Ice Rink" was printed with the menu of 37 Club's 20th anniversary dinner. The "Occasional Sonnet for Norman MacCaig" was published in *Chapman's* booklet *Norman MacCaig: A Celebration*. "Don Juan Retired" appeared in Cencrastus. Harriet MacIlwraith made a debut in *Literary Review*, and her sequence was afterwards published in *Chapman*.

The author wishes to express his gratitude to Derick Thompson, to Alan and Rae Riach, whose hospitality in New Zealand was the context of the title sequence, and to Tom Lowenstein and Sudeep Sen for comments on the manuscript.

Contents

Prologue
Northumbrian 1

Waking in Waikato
Hamilton, Waikato 2
Waking in Waikato 2
For Alan and Rae: Your Tree in Waikato 4
Thinking about MacDiarmid in New Zealand 5
'I Wanna Know – Everything' 6
Wellington Blues 8
Home Thoughts from New Zealand 9

Certain Opinions of Harriet MacIlwraith
10 — 19
The Affair of Hamish MacIlwraith:
Sequence in Absence 20 — 29

Autumn Poems
Borders 30
Soft Fruit Above Forfar 31
Truth in Edinburgh, August 30 32
September Starting 33
Crab 34
On the Far Side 35
Lothian 36
Missing You 36
The Found Displays 37
Edinburgh Gulls 37
Fear Sheep 38
Greeting, not Greeting 39
Grampian 40

Autumn Haikus	41
Night Hawks and the North East of Scotland's God	41
October Opera For Kate	42
Curling: Old Murrayfield Ice Rink	43
Hebridean	44
Turmeric Evening	45
November Nature	46
With Schubert and Schumann on the Eastern Front	46

Two Monologues

Don Juan Retired	47
Antony Fights Back	49

For Poets

RLS	51
Fourteen Line Poem Equals Sonnet	52
For Seamus Heaney, on his Nobel Prize	53
Remembering Paul Edwards	53
On the Death of Sorley Maclean	54
On the Death of George Mackay Brown	55
Occasional Sonnet for Norman MacCaig's 85th Birthday	55
For Jack Mapanje	56
Meditation on Mohammed Azharuddin	57

Elegies

Horn Play	59 — 63
At Warriston Crematorium, before Tom Scott's Funeral	64

Prelude: Northumbrian

One
Flotsam on Alnmouth sands: bricks, breezeblock ...
Where did some terrible force shatter houses
across that sea or wreck a cargo ship?
Are they bits of Tyneside Blitz gradually worked
by currents northward?

On the grass verge of the sands, cement blocks,
once anti-tank devices, stand arrayed
to spare the golf-course from erosion
by that slower invader, the long tide.
This beach is a moment's respite, no reward.

The world owes us nothing, truly gives nothing,
shrugs off our frenzies, will shift cemented bricks.
No dwelling or course endures. Yet the sand seems
                                                bountiful,
fickle light plays its glorious tricks.

Two
Gulls from below are sordid scavengers.
Hitchcock was right. They could be dangerous,
divebombers, ravagers.
But seen from above, in neverwas evening light
from a cliff above Craster,
their whiteness is like that attributed to angels,
there is woodwind elegance in their flight.
It's impossible just now to sense disaster
(which they'd survive anyway, like the sun).
Whatever the final score may be, we've won.
We are as if on that coast of Bohemia
to which mind's Vltava flows triumphantly,
under blue where the green imagined is no dream,
over sea south of Spitzbergen, north of Prague, all seas.

Waking in Waikato
(for Alan and Rae Riach)

Hamilton, Waikato

Now, here's a quiet city
near where the treaty was signed
before the battles raged.
There was never pity
only wills resigned
to faithlessness assuaged.
Stores downtown are well-stocked.
Restaurants, people say,
are latterly, sometimes, OK,
but propriety's not mocked
yet much. The Kiwi way's
subdued: there's the glad "hellay"
from everyone: few firearms are cocked.
Road deaths at Christmas – everybody's shocked.

Waking in Waikato

Dawn roars
and it's a stranger.
Wind and rain –
Antipodean dawn
speaks danger.

Lace curtains billow –
possibly here
a Scot shot a Maori,
here, under
my pillow

as it were –
yet it could be it was so.
Windy dawn
reminds me I transit here,
as it were, in-verso.

Clover white
on the green lawn
says it's all right,
travellers aren't
forlorn.

But the wind tears in –
from New Hebrides?
(Vanuatu now)
from Antarctica? –
sweeping fears in

James Cook, James Cook –
that second forbidden tree
you ate from
stands where hate, and love,
come from.

For Alan and Rae: Your Tree in Waikato

Your friend Lester, as a true Kiwi
objected to that thrush
which sings dawn and evening
at the very top of the huge tree
seen from your garden.

You say you're sorry you have
no panorama,
but I would settle for that tree instead
of any landscape.
It gives focus, like great drama.

One guesses at vast roots hidden behind those houses.
Its strong, long branches strike greenly
towards all corners of sky:
and the thrush, too,
concentrates thought keenly.

Alien bird it may be, but its preachment
is in all languages. I think
your toddler with his babble
probably talks to it:
yabadaba, yabadaba.

And the tree itself surges
as if all our forebears
rushed back through its branches,
with one bird to speak
for all of them, and all our urges.

Thinking about MacDiarmid in New Zealand

There are no raised beaches here: plenty of stones,
but few ruined buildings. The air is clear,
a palish blue. The birds which sing in it
are often of breeds imported from UK,
tweeting their insults over Maori bones.

And the Englishness! Recreated for fear
that something would be lost: and what was lost
were uniquenesses here that Anglos, even now, grieve –
local brilliant birds in retreat, Polynesian
ways in which people and landscape might cohere.

In glacier-like millennia, "New Zealand" 's a minute
dependent on what a handful of whites could thieve.
We all have little time to count the cost
amid the flowers, the bright and scented day –
so little time to dream better, try to begin it.

But what you, Chris, Hugh, were trying to say –
does that work here, however briefly, a blink?
Over such a distant border can we reive
capacity to enjoy what we think,
making all possible worlds our prey?

Unlike your Shetland, here are telephones
and Big Macs of little consequence. Friesian
cattle have done well. Kiwis (a fruit) make cash.
The story was hell, a steamy, brutal clash
of opposites past all appeasing.

Yet, living in this upside-down year
with persons falling, as everywhere, through time's sieve,
as one watches children brown and white at play,
although we'd find it extremely hard to pin it
down, there's something for you here, Chris Grieve.

It's a syncretism with its special tones,
with some kindliness grudgingly following great fear.
If there's a song, there's a million ways to sing it.
Languages always have something to say.
The firefolk sit in the sky on their Southern thrones.

'I Wanna Know – Everything'
(Kirk Douglas as Stanley Kubrick's Spartacus)

It's the craving for completeness that cripples one –
exactitude, plenity, "the full compass" –
as if one were to be quizzed by St Peter
and might not win through, at the gate, some pedantic
                                                          rumpus.

Whereas: all life is endured in bits and pieces,
the tiny local events which drive one frantic.
I said, "On our side of the Atlantic,"
and Alan said, "Which side of the Atlantic?"

Here in NZ the answer isn't perspicuous.
One could argue it both ways. What is clear
is that any answer is faintly ridiculous.
"Faintly" 's the right word. Small smears, we're here,
                                                          only here.

The globe bends and stretches away from, and to
the partial experience, the finite science,
possessed by me, possessed by you,
our brains on which we should have no reliance.

One hopes to light a lamp for several decades –
centuries even, better than under a bushel.
Meanwhile, hopping and squirming among the shades,
birds and worms swill the ashes of Bertrand Russell...

You go up to St Peter, you say, "I ask you, Jimmy,
whit the fuck could one man dae? ..."
And he says, "Fuck you, come on in," and you say,
                              "Fuck off –
I want away, I still want that plenity."

And flee back, perhaps, to the remotest point
of South Island, or the Northern Isles,
essaying to make everything conjoint,
while in some meridian, somewhere, some Buddha smiles.

Wellington Blues

Twelve storeys below my motel suite
a man in the street is singing the blues:
just one of the colours of this motley city
where Europe and oceans of difference fuse.
To concede to the blues would be a pity
when the sunset is salmon pink,
dark green vegetation bears deep red flowers
and Old World sham is further than people here think
on buildings, so many colours in any street,
not to mention the white of houses perched on the cliffs.
But what's the colour of these winds which power
themselves through Wellington in mighty riffs?
Blues are different here: the clean blue of sky
and a sense of vast distance conspiring to make one cry.

Home Thoughts from New Zealand
for Douglas

My Christmas here's more than half over,
yours has just reached you,
and I guess you're asleep, under cover
as snow brims the darkness.
Cold skin of a tangerine
in Santa's stocking
for children who'll wake soon in Scotland.
Here flowers are rocking
in butterfly breezes
and the seaside summons
while on besieged shores near you
the wind sniffs and wheezes.
I wish I could phone or fax to you
summer. My blue-sky thoughts,
tender about you,
wish your snug warmth could be brought
to hug my shirtsleeves –
not e-mail, feel-mail.
This verse is my silent *slainte*.
Towards you, I raise my chilled beer.

Certain Opinions of Harriet MacIlwraith

Born by accident in Saskatchewan from the liaison of a Wee Free clergyman and a Glasgow comedienne. Educated beyond perfection in Toronto, Boston, Geneva and Cambridge, she came to Scotland to pursue what pursued her. If she were in Who's Who she would give her hobby as 'living', her occupation as 'dying'.

She is told that she looks like an angel

Advertisements of virtue are redundant –
I laud that truism I cannot live.
As Franklin figured out,
socially speaking,
shy goodness is like water in a sieve,
cosmetics are the lively girl's best friend.
Muskily reeking,
falsely figured out
and lipsticked saint, I back to that dyed end
which makes both virtue and display redundant.

She displays her aptitude for theology

In the beginning there was Guilt. And Guilt
loved God, and God was always there with Guilt
– two fuddled together,
great boozing chinas –
and Guilt would back wee God up to the hilt,
poor little chap. 'Another double, God?
Nae drinks for minors?
Never mind yon blether!'
One night the poliss came and sussed out God.
Since then the bar's been lonely for old Guilt.

She recognises advancing middle age

If this dishonesty which furs the tongue,
devours the liver slowly, grates the brain,
could ask forgiveness
that would be wrung only
by the fact that it makes pain
making believe that the clear-eyed
cheer of the young only
should need forgiveness,
since that affirms so cheaply what's denied
by this dishonesty which furs the tongue.

She further considers the natural process of ageing

The rasp of whisky and the reek of sex
go well together now my ageing palate
demands lime pickle
breakfast, lunch and dinner.
Without such blasting I can't salivate,
no bacon's salt, no curry's hot enough.
That chill tickle
helps me stay a sinner
and celebrate what otherwise is rough –
the reek of whisky and the rasp of sex.

She revels in her own iniquity

'There may be covenant made with death and hell:'
Cromwell was right. I did that years ago.
Constrained to come to terms
with skull beneath pocked skin
I've lived for night, shunned noontide's bogus glow
and strictly acted on low moral levels
among life's basics – sin
and slime of cunt and worms.
So I've won through hot times with several devils,
at truce with death, domesticating hell.

She counsels against realism

'Better be wicked than ridiculous' –
I don't agree. I'd rather, far, be both
and am both anyway,
a sinner clowning towards death.
These ultra-realists, so very loth
to show they've 'hearts' like others, which are hurt
(nerves rather, twisted by short breath
or racked by *ennui*)
prove that all zeal to keep soup off your shirt
makes you less wicked, more ridiculous.

Unwonted contentment thrusts her towards regularity

Corralled by happiness, I kick and fume.
This filly was not meant to be so tame,
so newly rich
in smugness like a foal,
despised by Tragedy and snubbed by Shame,
avid for nothing I cannot consume.
It's neural itch
which surrogates for soul,
not smirks and snoozing lack of that self-blame
which, faking crisis, makes me kick and fume.

She gives encouragement to her latest lover

Since you believe in magic, you're in love
and swindle skin to light and night to day.
Ducking from ecstasy
some men prefer the sensible
hobbies which keep periculous gods at bay,
while others, chained by lust, disdain the tragic
and covet only sensual
bucking in ecstasy.
Refute their crassness, make me blaze with magic –
and then confess it's magic that you love.

Then she explains herself to him

Now that your spells lack efficacity,
now that your semen is no longer potion
but mucky stickiness,
I will refuse to regret
my venture of such wetness and emotion
as if Laphroaig were just its hangover,
Olympic Gold merely sweat,
our fucking wickedness.
I mouth your magic for another lover.
Your spells regain their efficacity.

She inveighs against the quiet life

Now you must greet disaster as a friend
who grabs your arm to halt you as you stroll
over the precipice
and so claws you
from that annihilation you can thole,
from self-love's indolent and easy end.
Sweirty lures you
with luscious recipes
you think you can afford and swallow whole
till next you greet disaster as a friend.

She further rejects the idiocy of rural existence

The piebald lapwing twits, and having twit
flaps round a little in the skinkling sun.
Dirty old Nature'
s up to all her tricks –
another snoring holiday's begun.
Blank country air's beguiling me again,
but urban nurture
soon will make me sick
of gulps of westwind softening the brain,
conspiracies of trees to make me twit.

Nevertheless, she begs to differ from David Hume upon the virtues of civil society

'Skin-clad and balancing on burnt-out logs' –
my old friend S.B. wrote that deathless line
about some Indians –
Red – she was suggesting partly
that noble savagery was pretty fine.
Burnt out, I think about it when the wine'
s running low at a genteel party,
civil opinions
exhaust me, and I wish the bourgeois swine
down some deep river, skin-full on slim logs.

She moves towards social commitment

There's so much more to life than solo piano
– let's whack the cymbal, summon up the brass.
Even a piccolo
teetering prettily
at least means the musician's off his arse
and might march militant behind some banner
twittering pithily
unlike that gigolo
who seeks to trap you in a narrow pass
where he's the maestro, you're the solo piano.

She celebrates Eros

My lack of any talent I can love
dejects me when I hear Domingo sing
with Abbado conducting
or watch Navratilova
on TV, lithe and strong when she is smashing
a little furry ball to life's far corner.
Ruefully, I'm perfecting
now my maiden scope is over
an attitude to outlob any scorner –
'I have no talent save the best one, love.'

She is reconciled with life by jazz in a pub

These jazzmen may be balding, but their horns
are generous with all youth ever was
and all maturity
should ever want to be.
Least mathematical of things is swing
which utters the definitive 'because
we're free and we are free
in perpetuity.'
Our earth has only seen one decent King,
Count, Duke or President – obey those horns.

She consents to summing up

I wail my still unfinished adolescence
as toenails blizzard on my way to death.
I'm forty now
so very soon, or late,
and taste the gravedirt in my teeth and breath.
As scum replaces what was effervescence
yet cravings don't abate
now calf is cow,
I must instruct myself I've learnt no lessons
and bop on through persistent adolescence.

She is nevertheless brought up short, epidemiologically

AIDS means I must increase my store of aids.
(The rubber barons bloat up in this boom.)
No more casual
easy screwing.
My apertures must close or make more room,
a greater gulf where muffled venture wades
after kissless wooing,
cautious razzle.
Quaint mimicry of decency must loom
to choke the thrust where laughter found its aids.

Understandably, she fantasises

A female Gilgamesh, I seek this barman
somewhere beyond the cinema's slick screen
who will pour out
purely celestial
peaty and aphrodisiac poteen
which there's delight and and never any harm in.
Then I'll be bestial,
blithely soar out
in skies where this creased body's never been
to hoochmagandie with the careful barman.

She bows out, differently from Chris Guthrie

It's only when you die you're absolute,
your name engraved in stone or merged in air,
the smile preserved
in celluloid,
the rant complete, the ruined choirs bare,
the cornet clinching with its final toot –
I tell you, Lord,
I've never swerved
from seeking out the wicked places where
pissed, screwed, I might foreknow the absolute.

The Affair of Hamish MacIlwraith

Biologically older than his half-sister Harriet, but emotionally a thousand years younger, Hamish, infected by Arminianism, attracted to Buddhism, has always sought salvation through carnality. The city of Edinburgh, where grey stone is transfigured by sunlight at any time in any season, stimulates his propensity to hope as surely as its chill winds under dark skies precipitate despair. What Hamish, a scruffy professional man, does for a day-by-day living is irrelevant to inner cycles affected by outward weather.

Sequence in Absence

*Qué importa que mi amor no pudiera guardarla.
La noche esta estrellada y ella no está conmigo.*

*Eso es todo. A lo lejos alguien canta. A lo lejos.
Mi alma no se contenta con habierla perdido.*

Pablo Neruda

Loss

When Nuala said that time, 'Life is about loss –
all about loss', I did not think of you
but now I do,
now I do.

The worst is that we come to terms with loss –
Time's meanest trick. What's special is forgotten
and that's rotten,
rotten.

I do not want to ease up and get over
loss of your unrepeatable swift loveliness
and soft caress,
oh, silk caress.

If we must part, I want to cheat bland time
and feel immediate loss of you forever,
every weather,
all your weather.

April Folly

If I mistake the pager in my pocket
for a spring songbird, darling, don't give me a rocket.
This is a strange season. The other night it snowed
in mid-April, an inch on the cars parked in my road,
but on the bushes like blossom. Then came rain
as raw as November. Since what's real is bizarre –
here in Edinburgh, at least – now that the sun is back
I adjure myself never to doubt your truth again.
Through astounding nature, you are just what you are.
Beyond prediction, I learn from you what I lack.

Of Bees

Little piebald beasties
graze Pat's compost.
These bees won't swarm.
They tumble and forage,
soon may bumble,
browse back to muck base.
These are home-bodies –

not hive but heap.
This sort give no sweetness
but may be less fierce.

From you my darling
I've had so much honey,
of course I worry
that you may sting.

Homing North to Edinburgh

I ride in a kind of cold fever
with a train ticket out of brick Suffolk
where white may on hedge is in fever.

I ache as a man who may never
be nursed by what he desires –
your voice and silk person forever.

Self cure is my soundest endeavour.
My city of stone will soon hold me,
where leafing resembles endeavour.

Yet stone cannot cool a cold fever
nor spring fail to stir gorse in Scotland
– reviving or curing my fever

despite or through my endeavour,
your absence or loving forever,
or rather till death stills all fever.

Eroica

You on that rock –
you wanted more than that.
Blizzards, gales, anything wilder
than the breeze off North Berwick.
Wilder than me?
We'll see.

Oh darling, darling,
I sense in you
lust to leave barracks, I catch
the whiff of men trained to kill.

I am a pacifist, haunted
by that photo of a German soldier
lunging into a village
in the Caucasus in 1942.
His eyes stare
like the air.

May Winds

Fickle Eros picks his time to strike –
Edinburgh freezes greyly in May and it's over.
My prophetic soul forewarned me in the chill wind.
Then you phoned and told me you'd picked another lover.

'Easy come, easy go?' Not easy and not gone.
You sounded notes in me never heard before.
Happiness never was the point, perhaps.
Mainly, it mattered that life meant more.

You came like a slow wind. Are you gone with the wind?
Fidelity and betrayal are faint specks
compared to the mountains, the sky and the wind of love
which surges and blurts and doesn't care what it wrecks.

Do I bin you as a folly, return to despair,
or settle sanely for life which means less?
No. I am grateful. I can't just wince and shrug.
I desire to weep, and yet I want to bless.

The Joy of Motoring

North of South it's not veldt. What? Steppe I suppose–
that high equatorial country not meant for walking
except by Africans. I drove at a mile a minute
over it, out of synch with the leopard stalking,

outpacing the cheetah: dry mile after dry mile
towards a dusty town, beer, and a laundered bed
with mosquito nets. In Kenya the sun goes down
at 6.30 prompt and insect song fills your head.

I could drive like this forever, I believed –
past Kilimanjaro, on and on and on
to where the standing rocks are Shona gods
past great Zimbabwe's wordless ruins, on.

But I wanted more than cold lager at the end,
more than a shower, the pleasant bedroom cool
shared with large spiders, the irrelevant book.
Only now have I realised that I wanted you –

tall, easing your pants down, your strong legs
surprisingly bruised blue – when did we do *that?*
We've gorged on brai, now your bra slips off.
Your litheness exceeds that of any great cat.

Defrag

I hate these poems since they fall between us,
wee factoids littered upon paper.
They do not correspond to your gorgeous body,
nor can they register the fact of my anger.

Defragged, I stood before you, floppy disks
in order. And the hard disk was sound, too.
I was reconstructing a messy life.
The upshot of this was meant to be you.

Or us, rather. That elusive us
which has been me, as far as I could find
me, now flickers like a pc going crazy.
The screen will crash. I think I have been blind.

Biffly Blues

Now I experiment with broken form,
being broken. There is a way of playing
behind the beat which Satch knew. I
can't do it.

Or maybe can 'replicate' – or likewise.
I am dazed. Nothing might work
but the sound of a horn – Red Allen maybe,
playing the blues.

'Biffly Blues' – Well, in the long run Red was dead.
'For Red, these words, for you, opposing time ...'
That's grandiose. I should seek humility,
be biffly.

Blackburn have won the league. The fans are happy.
You've chosen someone else. I'm very unhappy.
What more is there to say? I sign off
yours biffly.

Homeric

Now memory attacks me like a rocket.
Despite myself, I wince and shout.
I hate to brood on you but cannot stop it.
You thrill me as you throttle me with fright.
Your care, like Pallas Athene's, once
blazed bright.
Now your whim, like Aphrodite's
devours the night.

Coda

At the airport, flying south out of a small haar,
not expecting to see you, not knowing where you are,
I watch the cold trees sway in the pale mist
and I realise now that I was truly blest.

To have known you at all, to have seen you pee in my
                                                                                      sink,
to have experienced the ecstatic blink
most folk never know. To be honoured with my clan.
To have been, however briefly, your man.

Autumn Poems

Borders

Humped on a hillock
by Lynton Kirk
there's a graveyard
where you stare across to England.

Why is it that the mind
insists on borders
in the sweep of hills
under fine weather?

I think because we need
limits to the majesty
of Scotland's glaciated humps.

Otherwise we would be midgeted
by immensities of gorse, heather
sky forever.

Soft Fruit above Forfar
(in memoriam, PRC)

Faced north, in spite,
the oats have crisped
to a sussuration
and under dusty leaves
in the raspberry field
there are still a few
red peepers. Pick one,
hold it between thumb
and finger to scry it against
the whelming Grampians, blue-
patched grey vastness
of chaotic sky which spits
at the dry strath a little
wanted rain. Give thanks
to glaciers for nothing
more than sweet acid perishing,
muted brilliance, froward pips.

Truth in Edinburgh, August 30

Truth is not like these fagends
I tip in the dustbin
from the car ashtray.
Truth's not smoked out.

Truth differs from this morning's
Scotsman, instant history –
truth didn't happen yesterday.

Nor is truth like the grey roofs
seen through my office window,
spires and castle clearcut against sky:

the city's thousands submerged
behind stone, beneath stone,
even the traffic at this height dumb.

Truth is a child
climbing the Mound in rain
out of today into
tomorrow with effort.

September Starting

You think you could reach
across the Forth and touch
poppies in the Fife fields.

Roses appear huge as
cathedral windows.

Trees wear russet flecks
as if dressed up
for a night at the opera.

The light is so rich
with generous details

that a razory edge
of cold in the air
seems not so important.

Crab

Four crabs from the cold firth
alive for a shilling. The largest
reared in the pot, in spite of
the fierce water, but soon
we cracked his limbs with our teeth
and wheedled with spoons and fingers
for the last shreds of flesh
from the crannies of his briny body.

In that brittle maze
I found no features to remind me
of our brains, our livers
or our smooth bellies, yet doubtless
their functions were held by some part
of the paste of his cavities.

Spread, soup and risotto –
only the gills were rejected.

In the days we ate him
I did not forget
his moment on the floor
to amuse the baby, when she
gloated at the slow clash
of his last menace,
nor that shape which made me think
of a soft soldier
fried in the cockpit of a tank.

On the Far Side
(in memoriam, I.M.D.)

On the far side of fear
still beeches caress
the blind breeze.

On the far side of grief
potatoes are pulled from the earth
which is glistening on them.

The far side of love is where
tenderness spreads like a stain
drying, not dry.

On the far side of pain
a born child streams between flanks
trembling to stillness.

On the far side of despair
stones are lungs
at the brink of a cry.

Lothian

It would be the good childhood you never had.
The gold of sun and silver sea
that beckons deliciously out, the leaves of a tree
copper; on days which are never sad.

In imagination you have it as sun flares
on faces in Lothian Road this September,
shop girls and tourists – a childhood you remember
and never could have – no loneliness, no nightmares.

Missing You

It isn't just at the fine events
where I wish you were beside me
– great theatre nights, excellent movies –
but in the simplest acts, as when
I walk down a street in sunlight,
wish I could phone you, say it's a lovely day,
or when I cook and imagine you eating.

It isn't just the music we shared
which brings pangs,
it's all the tunes you may never have heard,
taped jazz at random in a bar,
fiddler and flautist at work anywhere.
Whatever voice sings or instrument utters
it is your name which they are repeating.

The Found Displays
for Polly Rewt

Where are they found these displays, but everywhere?
It's not that one thinks then plucks them out of the air.
With a suddenness they're always there ...

So one writes that and places it on the table
and the bartender lass comes round
and spots it ...

'It's very good, it's very sporadic'
she says with her pounce and poise and exceptional hair.
Trying to come up with a rhyme, I find 'gladic',
a word which may not exist but is part of the air.

Edinburgh Gulls

Riding inland on our peculiar winds
the gulls possess this city as of right.
They point blue sky, grey stone, with perfect white.

Pigeons who plod the pavements bickering
seem restive serfs under these lords of light,
finches mere flotsam of a moment's flickering.

Yet it's garbage gulls are after. Lower your sight
to spoiled, spilled binbags. A gull finds
fodder in squalor – so mean, so bright.

Fear Sheep

...Una oveja salvaje
lejos, en la región, lame el color helado
de una piedra... Neruda, 'El Corazon Magallanico'

Grey dawn.
I tilt into my jog.
Sheep, colour of sky
flock off my path
bleating the wind I lean through.

A mile further on
this outlandish
heraldry, fieldful
of hell sheep feeding
in profile, still
as ghost plaster.
Qué pasa?
I think I am dead
till, closer,
I see their jaws move.

Terror of sheep!
those identical bland
spook faces,
middle-class masks upon nullity –
wool should be cold.

"Patagonia, there, so
distant, a wild
sheep is lapping the frozen
tint of a stone ...
Desolation alone rules."

But this is West Lothian. Sun
glows in russet shalebings, gleams
green in canal skin, warms
reaffirmative brown fur
of a run-over bunny.

Greeting, not greeting
for Peta Sandars

To wake to the reassurance of grey stone streets
under a clouded, adequate Edinburgh sky,
finding one has the right change in one's pocket
for once: and for once there seems no cause to cry ...
It is unnecessary to fly on a rocket.
Here is a day which one greets, not greeting.

Grampian

North of Crieff, over cold rock
the land's bracken bosoms are golden.
"I think how an amethyst sunbird
sips minty flowers at evening

seeming light as the flowers ..."
An eight-year-past image for happiness
flickers from Africa, now
that I must replace it

seeing October Speyside's
maple gold, red-leaf rowan
glow through grey drizzle where trees screen
the cleft of a whisky burn's whispering –

labial soft waters,
leafslip and pine refreshment
windshaped above worn stone
in love's minute, unfinished.

Autumn Haikus

With a whoosh leaves drop.
Time should end
on such a clearskied
October day.

The trees have been saving up
for their golden robes
all the wet summer.
Now they divest themselves
quick strippers
with an austere Franciscan fervour.

Life should stay like this
for ever –
luxurious sky: repentant trees.

Night Hawks and the North East of Scotland's God
for Joy Hendry

It is as if the world is a Hopper painting,
the light as chill as that and as strangely warm.
There is an absence somewhere which hates us
but also a motherhood keeping us from harm.

There are always the new words and the new time coming,
dancing with iambs and dactyls not yet expressed.
Out there, always, the humming birds are humming.
Tomorrow night we will show up properly dressed.

October Opera For Kate

Gotterdamerung on the radio –
the crazed Valkyrie
hurls herself into the flames
as the Gods' home crumbles.
A dwarf greets over gold.
Fishy maidens triumph.

We were both of us right
to mistrust Wagner
I think, as I plod
through this slow autumn.
(How long green lingers
on the trees this year.)

Mozart's the man – 'They're all like that',
'Pardon, Countess, pardon' – transitional
quick emotions survived, not
self-immolation
after hero-sized betrayals –
but cynical, not so?

Somewhere in between
there's the ground no opera occupies,
where music's the laughter
of a child on a seashore,
where a well-cooked meal
sustains as arias don't.

Brunnhilde burns as stews shouldn't.
A hurt child can afford no pardon.

Curling: Old Murrayfield Ice Rink

Ice-capers! Time cannot stale
our pot-bellied skittishness. Watch us
frisking like penguins who've guzzled
too many tunas
off Tristan da Cunha. But who
dares lampoon us? Directed
by skeely skips, we address
elementals with modest finesse.
Not 'bowls on the rocks' this, but stones
over ice: final realities.

Ice in captivity, certainly,
stones smoothed to human shining,
but heavy
real stones. See them sinuate
target-wards suavely.

Truly this joust has more import
than slim-shanked cavortings across there
by teeny-bopping, insouciant
easy
skaters.

Sweat, greybeards!
Concentrate. Sweep
hard, harder –
we might
        yet
                win.

Hebridean

You are the wood I wander in.
I can find no way out of you.

Here are the bones
of the deer we dined on.

Glimpsing another deer
I lack your sure aim.

These berry bushes
will bear fruit again next year.

This is a glade where we slept
when the sun was warm.

They are silent now,
the birds which sang in summer.

Even squirrels shiver.
Night is falling.

I will lurch past needling branches,
through frosted bracken,

till darkness lifts to reveal
the wood I abide in,

waiting for birdsong,
impatient for next year's berries.

Turmeric Evening

Old curry days return
with a whiff in the street: garam masala ...
We burped in from the bar
to hog huge beef biryanis,
students with potent appetites,
no palate.

Glimpsed maybe balding now,
across traffic, from enough
distance to make them clear,
guys who weren't just younger then
but bristled with striking
youth, impertinent –

now plumped out with expenses,
smoked by careers' exhaust,
pigeon-streaked with credit deals, uncharismatic
connoisseurs of posh claret, yearn perhaps
back to virgin girlfriends and hopeful rubbers
in skint wallets.

It's still the same corner,
though shop signs have changed
and the restaurant now purveys
subtle jalfreezies, scant portions with names
unkent by we lads who went
burping and blurting.

We speak. It's the same wince
in each pair of eyes. He's grey.
Am I less grey? His teeth are still good.
Here's a five o'clock sizing –
thirty odd years since,
now this turmeric evening.

November Nature

Wangrass late autumn when the northwest gale
assaults from Greenland flailing wet whale fists
some stubbornness within frayed leaves resists
not yet, not yet, as we do though we squint
and curse, waiting the bus from which we'll see
the bleak firth, breakered, smack Queensferry's quay.
The Forth Bridge tholes. Cars aren't flushed hurtling off it.
Like live wood, metals haven't felt their limit.
One frail thing seems to be the human mind
conjecturing surprise about all this –
but thought's in nature too, with boats which jump
and slant and haven't slipped their moorings yet.

With Schubert and Schumann on the Eastern Front *for Omer Bartov*

The word one is fishing for is not pathos or pity.
Forgiveness is condescension. There is the point
where it's as if one was cheerful or witty ...
Love is the word. But the times have been out of joint.

You have frozen with your friends on the Eastern Front
on both sides. What they did was very wrong,
to put it mildly. But mildness is part of the point.
The horror dissolves into sentiment and song.

As the great late Roddy McMillan said, there's good
sentiment and bad. We must cherish the good,
work every day on believing in the good,
be fond of what is beyond pathos or pity.

Two Monologues

Don Juan Retired

Signor Diavolo, lord of the lusts of night
and of the lists which my servant kept in his bag
I write to thank you for your many favours
soliciting one more, but little trouble, I hope.

That charade was efficacious which I designed
and with your kind assistance executed.
Even my frock coat was barely scorched –
not that I need it now: I wear Shetland sweaters.
They will never find me here. There is no phone,
and in any case I have changed my name (to George Gordon).
For the superstitious, your fumy kingdom is real,
my supposed fate there just. For you and me, sir,
there is the certainty of nothing
and till then, such as I have now, material goods –
excellent smoked fish and oatcakes, preserved berries,
a view of the sea, a select library
of eighteenth century authors, a few cassettes
and the conversation of an intelligent doctor
not too addicted to my Glenlivet whisky.

I am writing a treatise on the disease of love,
those symptoms affecting women who see in a man
anything more than an apparatus
for titillation, perhaps for begetting of children,
and those which persecute men who will not acknowledge
that after three women, the fourth is no surprise
and cricket statistics can be just as exciting.
Its publication (my pseudonym will be 'Freud')
should cause a stir. Experience counts for something.

But I shall read no reviews. I shall promenade
after tea to the pier, to enjoy the subtle colours
of gloaming on this far north-eastern shore –
ungolden yellow, a grey which is almost blue.
I appreciate the skills of guillemots,
cormorants, gulls, who never drown
and defend their nests with the fury of such
as wish their genes to survive in the brisk air.

A woman serves in the bar who meets my needs
absent-mindedly: her disease
was a fisherman drowned in the great storm,
since when she appreciates fellowship under blankets
without illusion. Her coffee surprises me
by its quality, so far from the cities.
It will be warm through the approaching winter.

I do not ask how those Donnas yammer, yammer
nor seek news of the appetites of Fraus.
My evidence is complete. I prefer
to listen to Telemann, or a wader's cry.

There is one of your servants, however, I must hear of.
She who betrayed me. The one who never bored me.
In what elegant cafe now, wearing the furs
of what rich and complaisant husband, does she sip
the best of Mocha with a glint in her eye
nimbler than the flash of an oystercatcher?

I await your reply. I cannot disguise this,
with as much impatience as is possible
in a man who savours Glenlivet and writes
in a calm circle of anglepoised light,
Gibbon beside him, prudently double-glazed
against sea-hurling storms which will drown no gulls.

Antony Fights Back

Hercules is my god, after all.
I've felt him in my prospering arm
on fought fields where prompt dust
fixed blood, blotted, in very clearcut
shapes of disaster for others.

It's the fresh mornings I crave
when I might spear a gazelle
in a long gallop off the route of march,
then, in the dry lands, scoop from a puddle
such as the dead beauty might have made itself
moisture to slake excitement's thirst.
But at noonday also I have kept going,
joked about my paunch to fainting youngsters,
till at last, in my tent, there was fresh roast game,
wine not too sour, then the sleep
of exhaustion purposeless since battles win
nothing save chance to lead in further battles
(and meanwhile to be generous to brave captains,
which is a purpose.) I could march to Thule
or up Nile to the Mountains of the Moon
contented merely to have marched and slept.

No sleep in Egypt. My queen commands
till nearly dawn, backgammon, for wagers,
and then, smelling of paradise, she taunts me
with the length of Caesar's cock, as I struggle
to stop her tearing mine off. We'll
be drunk again by noon. What
held me here, while I imagined
that fresh north ocean
which Caesar sailed on – it breeds

fine oysters and also rumours of mines
further north, among painted men? Herself
of course, but why her when others,
queens in deportment if not in name,
have panted after me through Rome, a city
not so austere as my gypsy thinks?

It's this, I conjecture, as I pledge my paunch,
my wheeze, my bleared eyes, towards the capital –
Africa. Huge tusks of ivory
handled into Alexandria. Slave girls
of jet nude sheen under the dust of travel.
And a drumming such as Thrace had never matched,
heard once, as my quick queen, taken with it,
hopped in a public square at noonday. Tokens
of realms too far from Rome
which I'm too old to conquer, pastures
which I'll never hunt on. There's an odour
the Nile sweats out which might have flowed
from the source of all crotch-moisture, every perfume.

While Roman politics blockades the south,
my lean past hauls me coldwards. That small queen
can be the only Africa I'll have.
To save myself, I sail tomorrow
from this continent I'd march on and then sleep in,
then die, a dampness in the dust, be
like the urine of gazelles dried
almost at once by the triumphant sun.

For Poets

RLS

Beauty and fear: the long remembered faces,
childhood nightmares, far, far ago ...
Wind clatters through the streets of Embro
with the devilish horseman whose demands we know
and the lost answers of the hollow places,
wind always asking what we owe, what we owe.

Biscuit and silk, bought skin from the Grassmarket,
whores blurted out at, far, far ago ...
The devil inside the achieved person
goads the child of sorrow, acquainted with woe,
who puts queer questions to the smooth faces
of Embro professors, smart, so low.

Enormous Pacific, ocean skin wrinkling
beneath vast dawn – a long way to go
to meet new devils with their different masks,
cryptic creatures whether friend or foe,
flowered maidens with barely expressible graces,
where you dream of grey Embro, long, far ago.

Fourteen line poem equals sonnet

*for Ken Arvidson, Sano Malifo,
Sudesh Mishra, Alan Riach*

A sudden colloquium: poets in the bar
behind the Robert Burns Liquor Store
in Hamilton, Waikato, NZ.
Burns would have loved it:
to traverse like that
over poetics and politics –
the iamb, Ackroyd's Dickens and ▬▬ ▬'s
murder of Ken Saro Wiwa in your sights.
There was a special depth of focus
as you ranged from Samoa to Scotland,
from Naipaul to Fiji,
and a fifth person, myself, limped beside you,
while the world, for the length of four beers,
paused on its axis.

Sonnet for Seamus Heaney on his Nobel Prize

'Sook' is a word we have here:
'Brownnose' is more widely used.
I hope I can honestly say 'just thrilled'
to be one of the intimate people to cheer –
'Intimate' meaning the first time I saw
your verse in a student bookie we both were in
I thought, 'Fuck, this guy will write us all out of sight.'
You'd begun and the rest of us had still to begin.
You were the spur: you were also the goad,
the example which inspired and which killed:
and of course I am still beginning ...
But I cheer, as if at Lansdowne Road,
because decorum has not been abused,
because the right team are winning.

Remembering Paul Edwards

We have to work past the edges of words.
How do we find a rhyme for pain?
The most obvious thing to talk about was Wordsworth.
Thank you so much, so much. I hear you saying
"Here's a partial terminus for your pathos and patience.
Sit at the desk with poetry.
Come in out of the rain."

On the Death of Sorley Maclean

chan eil ach coimhthional nan nighean
ag cumail na coiseachd gun cheann*

Sunset persists in the west
though its light is altered.
A shade is departed
from the rainbow of language,
yet words survive and those tones
like Atlantic breakers
which never cease their returning,
and thrash of branches in wind,
deciduous, evergreen.
Now, fighter and man of voice,
he keeps pace beside
the girls who go arm in arm
forever up and down
the lost loans of Hallaig.

*There is only the congregation of the girls
keeping up their endless walk.
Sorley Maclean, 'Hallaig'

On the Death of George Mackay Brown

Death was bound to come. The great generation is going.
People don't live for ever, and there were
so many of these, the pizzaz Scottish makers –
no wonder they seem to drop now like flies
in autumn. *Timor mortis* ... But it's spring
as George Mackay Brown
would always have been the first to remind us.
there are new generations, regenerations.
We'll be gone before they are consummated.
There is a bitterness in April
passing, the eternal loss of daffodils
but also the sweetness of young faces
which competence and majesty will fill
as they make new worlds out of remote places.

Occasional Sonnet for Norman MacCaig's 85th Birthday

About your minor manner
critics might fail to be judicious
but your voice doesn't whimper or stammer.
It speaks of the bodeful or delicious
with sly gravity, gallows not gallus joy.
Sub specie aeternitis,
your world is stern, not a toy
for a poetaster, for gossip at parties –
yet it's a pleasure. Words snare and extend the fun
as they puzzle at complexities,
gavotting amid pandemonium.
Between despair and ecstasy they steer
a steady post-Calvinist walk, an observant track
to seamy howffs where there's excellent crack.

For Jack Mapanje – a sonnet in reverse

I practised reading you out once to Shostakovich.
This got submerged under other itches.

You're the man who made our diurnal
lives seem petty
but who'd be so embarrassed that he interfered,

the politest of callers
on our consciences,
best poet ever to deprecate himself,

prime witness of our century –
the worst yet. We've
been blest by what for you was curst:

your endurance, those imprisoned years
when a strange, beloved bird
chirped in our lives.

Meditation on Mohammed Azharuddin
for Sudeep Sen

Azhar's out for a duck before I switch on the TV ...
What a pang. As splendid Tendulkar smites on,
I consider the love you and I share, Sudeep,
for the art of Mohammed Azharuddin,
a sizeable man with a serious face
and wrists which whip the ball
past point or through midwicket
faster than sound, though his feet aren't in the right place.

Have you ever yourself made moments like those,
timing a stroke out of time? Once – in Surrey I think –
I went out to bat with a lourd hangover,
lunged at my first ball, and it flew
just over the fast bowler's head, never high,
for a flat six ... Of course, I was out soon after.
Told of myself, such stories tickle laughter,
as if a bad poet had written a great line
(some do), or the least experienced cook
had executed a perfect Pavlova (might happen).

Art's nowise élite. A child can paint
a definitive picture. Unaccompanied song
from an untrained voice may be entirely beautiful.
Like Azhar's, all our imitation, practice,
revision, response to advice and nasty critics,
merely frame (if we're in form) the swift gift
of verb or rhythm which pushes words not there but
there, like a perfectly placed stroke in cricket.

Christians speak of Grace,
Zenpersons of one hand clapping.
I don't think of orgasms, which are usually worked for,
or the well rehearsed climax of a great Mass,
but of something finished at once yet in time without end,
as when my daughter, aged three,
held up bits of breakfast, declared,
'Here is a boy called Toast and he is looking
for a girl called Friend', or what a colleague confided
of unlikely late love, 'As soon as she came in,
and our eyes first met, we knew.' Can
what is given so randomly matter?

It has to, or we're bust, and life is nothing
but genomes jogging between dark and dust,
soiled carryout cartons in the gutter,
instant clichés coined and proudly quoted,
and tea sipped doucely behind lace curtains by noted
connoisseurs of bread and butter,
while, half heard, the TV news
says, "India's captain soon left, out for a duck."

Elegies

Horn Play

an elegiac pastoral

One: I.M. Peter May, d. 28.12.94

You play therefore you are: I write therefore I am.
Writing is play: your playing makes me write.
We are the moments we have been together,
days out of time, creating our own weather,

and out of time, or in that real time,
not pettifogging minutes, but the true
time which stands still, as if forever,
May walks out to the wicket, shy and clever.

Oval my paradise: a sheening green,
May in his perfect whites, his long sleeves buttoned –
that cover drive will flow, I know it will.
It whacks the boundary board, I hear it still.

As fast as Azharuddin's or Kanhai's
most wristy shots, most perfect executions,
May's drive, the body leaning with no violence,
speeds over Paradise: one hand claps: silence.

Our different kinds of play are all we are
worth having – moments when the timing works,
as when May's forehead rises with his eyes:
six over deep mid on, time beyond lies.

Siegfried goes down the Rhine towards the crash
of middle-Europe in mid-century.
Wight, a neat black man, catches Peter May,
the cover drive an inch above the grass.

Oh willow, willow – Tricky Sam is wailing
above a distant delta, plunger mute ...
Strange fruit: May tried to play ball with apartheid.
I find no rhyme in that, nor reason either.

Rhyme falters, the clock ticks and Egypt dies.
Lungs wheeze, legs fail, all facts are ash and error.
You play the simplest exercise – my heart
(a metaphor) is flushed with timeless art.

The contradictions can't be reconciled
within clock time. That art resolves one issue
is never proved. Forgiving Peter May
I can say this, though – you must play and play

'for tenor, horn and strings', for other horns,
for Miles, for Brain, for Hodges and for Grace
and Ranjitsinhji, batsmen now the air
we breathe: you must play, because you care.

Natural and classical or modern, let
that ripeness ooze as only you can make it.
Most elegiac of all instruments
the horn subsumes our lost, and found, contents.

Two: Rajshahi

Osim and Sohel, Mahmun and Asit
down by the Ganges where the grey mud
sucking at sunset matched my grey hair, grey shoes:
you are a combination that can't lose,

in memory, if not in fact. In time
and out of time, you hire a boat –
small fish in the bilges as the sun goes down:
I sit astern like emperor or clown.

There is no other sun than this red ball,
no other life than this: breath's all we'll get.
Sage eld and ardent youth are now confused.
I'm using you, and by you I am used ...

For what, though? Oh, of all things I prefer
things used and worn, as Brecht said, but I see
lads at the starting point, all sleek and new
(that's Yeats) and wonder what I offer you.

Hope? Like the blazing pull that wee left-handed
bat played on the strath as we drove here: splendid
as Sobers or as Gower in their primes ...
I fear that lad, though, will endure hard times,

six unrecorded, life reduced to mud. –
But, oh, those vivid pictures on rickshaws.
Bright saris on poor women's bodies gloat,
as we do, on the Ganges, just afloat.

For a few takas as sun sets we get
a lakh of rupees, red and glowing wealth.
Mud washes down the river towards ocean
as we delight in motion and emotion.

Three: I. M. Davie Cooper, d. March 95

Beats one beats two beats three beats four beats five –
that Davie Cooper feints and glides and jinks.
The ranks of Jambos can't forbear to cheer
though it's against them, this sweet goal he sinks

when driving almost to the line, he pots
at a fifteen-degree angle. Henry Smith
the goalie can do nothing. Tynecastle erupts
and Davie Cooper dances into myth.

The best of all, Rude Gullit said – he'd know.
Pele said that of Best, so aptly named,
Best let his gift die: Davie's really dead.
Aged 39, Gods loved him, he was claimed.

I dread that you, my love, might be so sudden.
Beauty like yours, envied by Aphrodite,
Pallas Athene might decide to clutch
up to the starscape, soaring past the flighty,

the lipsticked and the perfumed and mascaraed
uncertain and confused poor women, those
who substitute cosmetics for directness,
nudge intellect to smalltalk, sex to pose.

Davie at best was like our dawn in bed
when time's away and somewhere else. We move
as if defences don't exist except
as shadows of the excellence we prove.

In fact, there's no defence, there's no attack –
a pure compliance, as if Smith in goal
had summoned Davie to his line, as if
Hearts needed Cooper to make fortune whole.

Sandy, beside me then, denies it now,
says that he didn't will that Rangers score,
But he did, I did, everyone there did.
Now Scotland mourns that we will see no more

like that, like Coop, that selfsame excellence,
handsome and strict, his own man, wouldn't go
to England, Europe even, so Clydebank
and Motherwell and Ibrox know they owe

a grieving in return. Like perfect love
when best is given, nothing but the best
should be riposted. After so much bad faith,
such wrong turns, it's with you I've come to rest

I hope. Though Siegfried didn't. Down the Rhine
he came to be betrayed. And served him right –
crude hero, he had none of Davie's polish:
whereas your star would ornament the night

and when I hear you playing Siegfried's horn
all heroism's purged, there's no bad faith
possible, just for that time, at all,
ever again. I watch now Davie's wraith

dance excellently through the dazzled shades
of all the hard full backs, the cynic foulers –
beauty and innocence and honesty
as in the movements of midsummer bowlers

at evening on the green, old men and women
at ease with quiet pleasure, slowly proving
that the Gods may love those who die old
as we might darling, still replete with loving.

At Warriston Crematorium Before Tom Scott's Funeral
— remembering PRC and IMD

An August heat-haze hugs the heavy trees.
To say it's peaceful here would be to lie.
Amidst barelegged tourists good men freeze.
I shiver at the fact that we must die.

What good's the sunlight? Why is the grass green?
My dearest dead were burnt in this trim place.
I would betray them if I were serene.
Instead, I fumble for a lost, kind face.

I wronged you, father. It's long been too late
to make the slightest gesture of amends
for nights when we drank whisky sitting late
and I raged at you, though we'd wake up friends –

for my aiming to be different and failing,
aspiring to be different and succeeding.
"I love you" was the gist of all my railing.
On your live mind I was a vulture feeding.

And Billie dear, I've kept the walking stick
supported you in staggered years of dying
till suddenly you went – the cancer's trick
was: think your family settled, you'd stop trying.

Your last words to me – "No one listens
to me any more." But living folk aren't heard,
sick or hale, by atheist or Christian.
Of all they say, we never grasp one word.

It's when they're ash they infiltrate the brains
and settle on the nerves of those they leave.
We catch the undertones and sense the pains
of kind ones we no longer can deceive.

Soon there'll be music, poetry in there
as a muckle makar's ferried into fire
by electricity, not Charon: queer
it's dismal Hades that we should desire

rather than nothing. Now clouds mute the sun
but as noon nears, the heat's still thick and sweaty.
A bagpipe starts up. Keening has begun.
My brooding, soon, will seem, to others, petty.

Can mighty music help me mourn the whole
of humankind and reconcile me
to frogmarched parting from this light, this air,
sharp lyrics split me from bad self, beguile me

into a commonalty past despair
where stone and fire fight from pole to pole,
where merest chance to see the earth seems fair,
to count some tides in where vast waters roll?